# CALVIN DIDN'T KNOW

## Stephen E. Randall
With illustrations by Gel-oh

Copyright © 2006 Calvin Didn't Know by Stephen E. Randall.
Copyright © 1992 A World Without Color by Stephen E. Randall

ISBN: 978-0-9767189-3-2

All rights reserved. No part of this book may be reproduced or transmitted in any form or by any means, electronic or mechanical, including photocopying, recording, or by any information storage and retrieval system, without permission in writing from the copyright owner.

This book was printed in the United States of America.

**To order additional copies of this book, contact:**

Better Day Publishing, LLC
11152 Westheimer #341
Houston, Texas 77042

www.betterdaypublishing.com
contact@betterdaypublishing.com

## Contents

Prologue ........................................................................... 1
Epilogue ......................................................................... 31
Glossary ......................................................................... 34
African-American Inventions and Inventors .................... 35
Biographies of Selected Inventors .................................... 37

For Dolores, Brandyn, Vickie,
Lauren, and Heather C.

**Prologue**

This is Calvin. He is a 25-year old man who works as a mid-level manager for a medium size corporation in downtown Atlanta, GA. It is a typical Friday afternoon at work and Calvin finds himself looking forward to heading home for the weekend. What Calvin doesn't realize is that his life is about to take a very interesting turn. Lets take a look. . .

**Calvin Didn't Know**

Calvin was tired. This had to be the longest Friday he could remember. Meeting after meeting ... all day long. He missed breakfast because he had a meeting to attend; no lunch — another meeting; now here it was, three o'clock in the afternoon and he had to go to still another meeting!

"What is this one about?" he asked his secretary.

"It's a planning meeting for Black History Month," she replied.

Fuming, Calvin left the office. "Black History Month ... please. Why me?" he thought. "I'm not Black. What do I care about Black History Month?"

"Oh well, a job's a job," he murmured as he stepped into the meeting.

**Stephen E. Randall**

"Thank you for allowing me just a brief moment to address you. I am Dr. Carter G. Franklin, named coincidentally after the founder of Black History Week, Carter G. Woodson (The Father of Black History). Black History Month is a time when…"

**Calvin Didn't Know**

And that's all Calvin heard. He did all he could to pay attention but burn-out had set in. The next thing he knew the meeting was ending.

"Thank you for your time and consideration," said Dr. Franklin. "If I can be of any further assistance in your planning efforts, please don't hesitate to contact me."

As the group applauded, Calvin made his way to the door. "Great presentation," he said as he passed Dr. Franklin. "I really appreciate your coming. This Black history stuff is really very interesting."

**Stephen E. Randall**

"I have got to get out of here!" Calvin thought as he rushed to the parking lot and sped off. Arriving at home, he pulled his car to the curb in front of his house and headed inside.

"Oops!" he said to himself. "I almost forgot to set out the lawn sprinkler. It's supposed to be a hot one tomorrow." With that, he placed the lawn sprinkler and the hose in the yard, turned on the water and went into the house.

As he stepped into the house, Calvin almost tripped over the ironing board. But, too tired to put it away or to even climb the stairs to the bedroom, he moved it to the side, folded out his couch bed and jumped in.

**Calvin Didn't Know**

"I still can't believe I spent all afternoon helping to plan Black History Month," he mused as he started to drift off. "And I even obligated myself to attend an entire series of meetings to continue the planning. More meetings!! What a waste! I could have been doing something productive during that time span. Gosh, I wish there were no Black History Month. In fact, I wish Black people had never entered this country. Life would be so much easier." And with that he drifted off to sleep.

## LATE THAT NIGHT ...

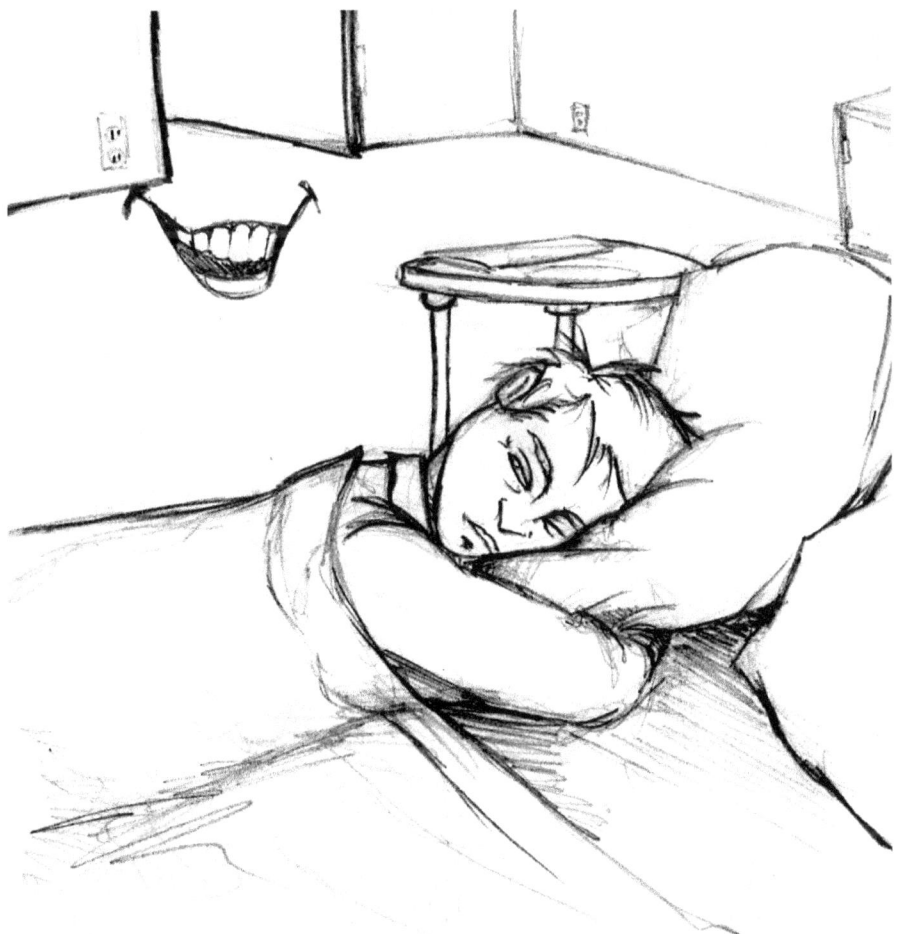

"Calvin!" a voice bellowed, waking Calvin from his sleep.

"What? Who's that?" Calvin said drowsily looking to see who was there.

"Calvin," the voice continued, "I am going to grant your wish. You are now in the United States of America, and no person of African descent has ever stepped foot in the country."

"Huh? Who are you?" Calvin asked as he awakened. Seeing no one, and figuring he was dreaming, he rolled over and drifted back to sleep.

**Calvin Didn't Know**

"OUCH!" Calvin screamed. "What in the world?" As he opened his eyes he saw his reflection in the stainless steel of the iron. Twisting to rise, he noticed that he was lying on the carpet. "What happened? How did I get here? The last thing I remember, I moved the ironing board out of the way so I could go to sleep on the couch bed."

"Calvin," a strange voice said, "I granted your wish. You no longer have an ironing board or a couch bed. They were invented by persons of African descent." (Ironing Board - Sarah Boone; Folding Bed - Leonard C. Bailey)

"Who is that?" Calvin said groggily. "And what are you doing in my house?" But there was no answer. Calvin, half asleep and extremely confused, sat up and reached over to the nightstand to turn on the light.

"No light either," the voice continued. (Electric Lamp - Lewis H. Latimer and Joseph V. Nichols)

"Who are you?" Calvin questioned as he tried to find the source of the voice. "What do you want?"

**Stephen E. Randall**

But he couldn't find anything or anyone. He reached for the clock to see what time it was. But the clock was gone as well.

"With no black people, no clock has ever been assembled in the United States," the voice continued. (First Clock Assembly - Benjamin Banneker)

Slowly waking up, Calvin stumbled to the window to open the curtains, tripped and fell through the glass. "What's going on here?" he thought to himself, fully awake for the first time.

"The curtains are on the floor, Calvin. The curtain rod was invented by someone of African descent. (Curtain Rod - S. R. Scotron) And you wished that Black people were never here. Remember?"

### Calvin Didn't Know

"A GHOST!" Calvin gasped, hearing the voice but seeing no one. Slowly, he raised his hand to his forehead. "I don't know what's going on, but it sure is hot in here. I must have forgotten to turn on the air conditioner last night."

"No, Calvin," the voice said. "The air conditioner and thermostat were both invented by a black person (Air Conditioner & Thermostat - Frederick M. Jones) — you wished Black people were gone, so the air conditioner and thermostat are gone with them."

"I have to get out of this house! It's haunted," Calvin said to himself. As he ran out the door, out of habit, he turned to lock the lock, but there was no lock there.

"The lock also," the voice taunted. (Lock - W. A. Martin)

**Stephen E. Randall**

"AAAAAAAHHHHHH!" Calvin screamed as he jumped from the porch into a pool of mud. Attempting to run, he tripped over the water hose as it ran into his front yard.

"Guess who invented the lawn sprinkler?" the voice echoed. (Lawn Sprinkler - J. W. Smith) "Ah, but it was your wish!!!"

**Calvin Didn't Know**

"I have to get out of here," Calvin gasped as he ran through the mud to the street. Jumping in his car, he turned the key, and the engine roared to life. He reached down to shift the car from "P" (park) to "D" (drive), but something was different. Someone had switched cars. The car Calvin was in had a stick shift. This wasn't Calvin's car. Calvin couldn't drive a stick!

"The automatic gear shift was invented by a black person, Calvin," the voice mocked. (Automatic Gear Shift - R. B. Spikes) "There is no automatic car now."

**Stephen E. Randall**

Reeling, Calvin rushed from the car, and ran down the street. "I have to get away from this voice," he thought. "I have to get away."

Calvin slowed his pace as he neared Main Street. "Something's different," he thought as he came to the intersection. "I just can't put my hands on it." Confused, but noticing a coffee shop at the golf club across the street, he warily stepped from the curb.

**Calvin Didn't Know**

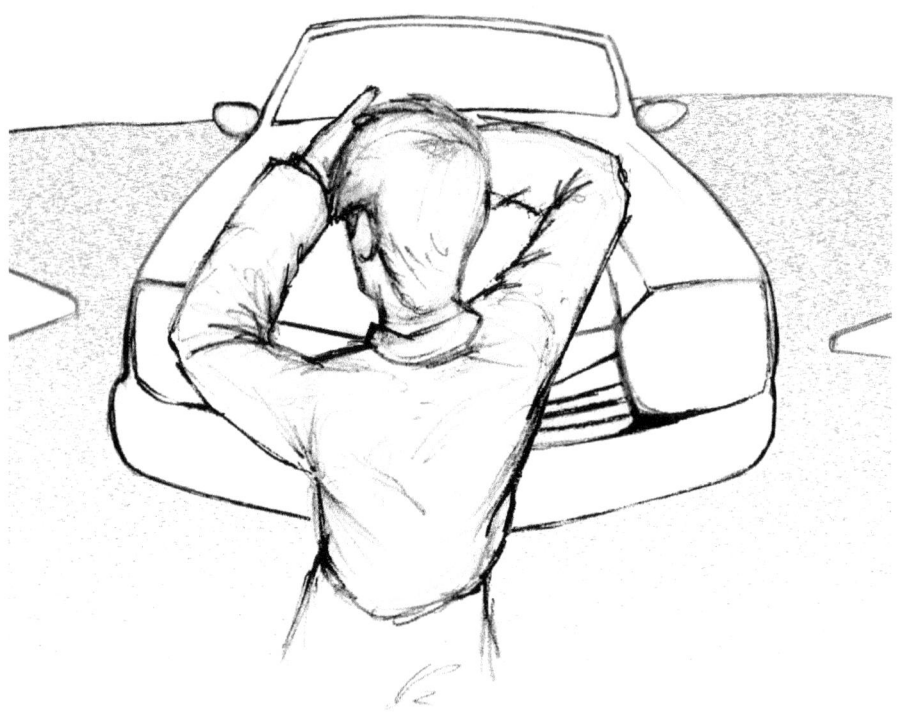

"Get out of the way, you idiot!!" a man yelled, swerving to miss Calvin by inches.

"Oh my," Calvin thought, "In my haste, I must have crossed against the light."

"There is no traffic light, Calvin," the voice said. "The traffic light was invented by someone your wish erased." (Traffic Signal - Garrett A. Morgan)

It was as if Calvin had been struck by lightning. Running with no obvious direction in mind, Calvin rushed into the street, directly into the path of an oncoming car. The last thing he remembered was sunlight reflecting from the hood of the car … and then pain … and then darkness.

Stephen E. Randall

### Calvin Didn't Know

*Although Calvin was the only person who wished for a country without African American people, many others were affected by the results of his wish being granted ...*

Dr. Peter Smith was approaching the first tee when he heard the crash. Dropping his club, he rushed over to see what had happened.

"Somebody call an ambulance!" a man yelled. "Somebody find a doctor, this guy's hurt bad," directed another.

"I'm a doctor," Dr. Smith gasped as he reached the corner. Seeing Calvin, he rushed to Calvin's side. "Call 9-1-1," he told the first person he saw. Then he immediately began to check Calvin's vital signs.

**Stephen E. Randall**

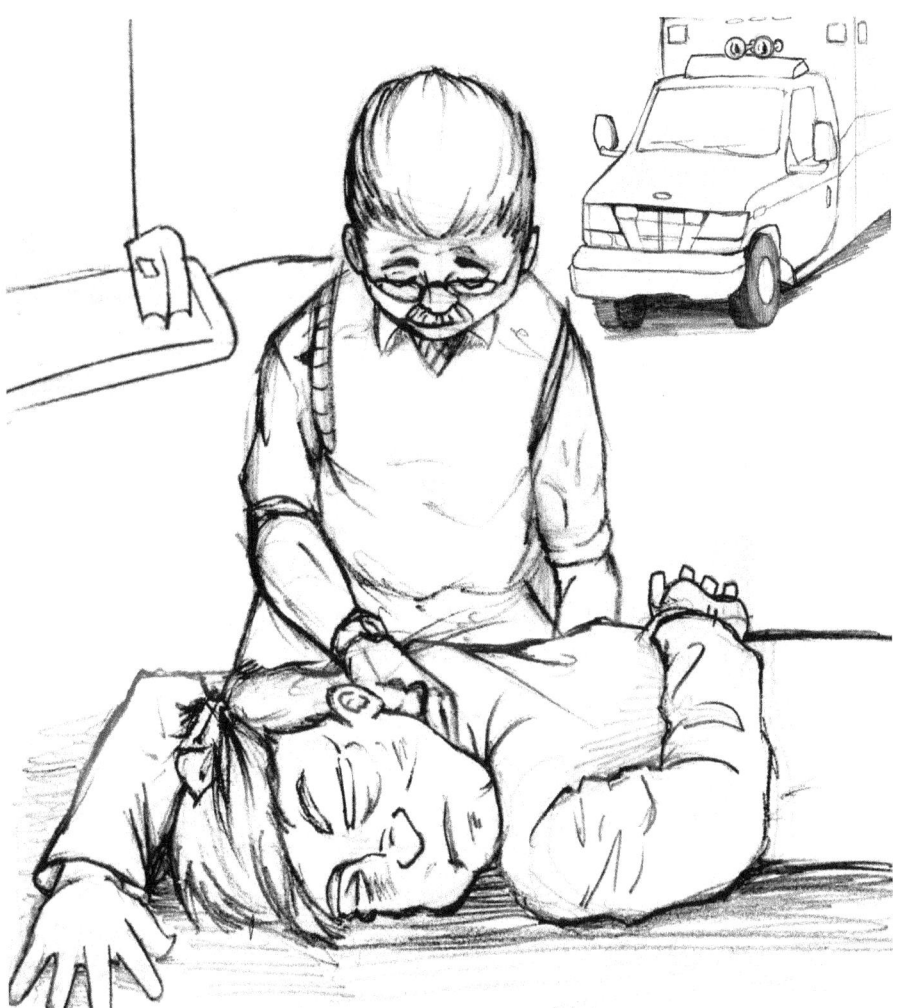

"Great! He has a pulse," Dr. Smith thought. "Now, where's that ambulance?"

Just then, the ambulance pulled around the corner. "What's the story?" the paramedics asked.

"The guy ran head first into a moving automobile," Dr. Smith replied. "He banged his head pretty bad, he may have a concussion, and he's lost a lot of blood. You guys take him to the hospital. I'll meet you there."

"This is the strangest day I've had in a long time," he thought when he reached his car. As he sped towards the hospital he began to reflect on the past few hours…

**Calvin Didn't Know**

Dr. Smith awoke Saturday morning after a very restless night. After a hot shower, he dressed in his riding clothes to prepare for a relaxing morning of horseback riding. Heading downstairs, he grabbed his favorite coffee cup, poured the freshly brewed coffee and reached for the sugar.

"What happened?" he wondered as his sugar poured out as a brown pasty substance. (Norbert Rilleux, an African American, invented the process for Sugar Refinement — but since Dr. Smith didn't make the wish, no voice told him what was going on.) "Oh well, no bother, I drink too much coffee anyway." With that, he grabbed his jacket and headed to the garage.

**Stephen E. Randall**

And there it was, his brand new, five-speed, candy apple red, Porsche 924 Turbo. The car of his dreams. He had even installed a special compartment in the trunk for his golf clubs. Hopping in, Dr. Smith turned the ignition and squealed down the street.

**Calvin Didn't Know**

He arrived at the stables a short while later and headed to stable #9, ready to saddle up and ride his favorite horse. But when he arrived he noticed something very strange. His horse was there, but someone had de-shoed the horse and stolen his saddle. Incensed, Dr. Smith rushed to the stable manager's office only to find fifteen other owners with the same complaint.

Stephen E. Randall

"Ladies and gentlemen I'm not sure what happened," the stable manager explained. "Somebody must have come in last night and taken the shoes off of the horses and stolen each saddle. It's almost as if the saddles and horseshoes disappeared into thin air. We are working hard to solve this mystery and will contact you upon its resolution. Please accept our apology." (Saddle - W. D. Davis, Horseshoe - O. E. Brown)

Dr. Smith was puzzled. "Why would anyone steal just saddles and horseshoes," he thought to himself. "Something strange is going on."

## Calvin Didn't Know

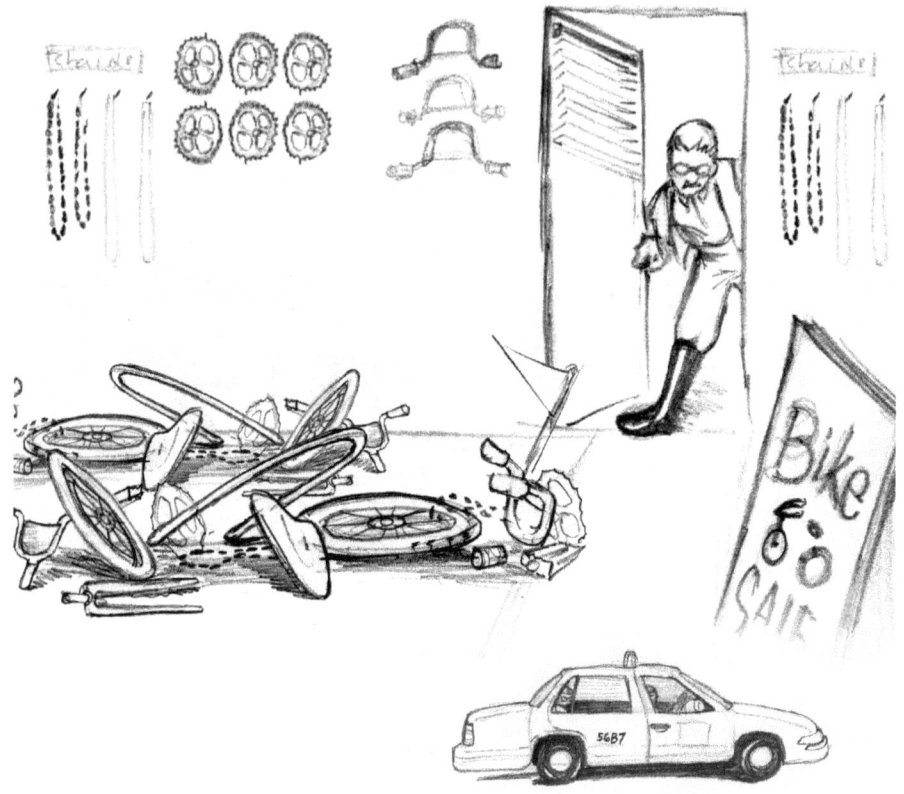

As he headed home, Dr. Smith noticed a new sign, BICYCLES RENTED ... CHEAP!!!

"That's it," he thought. "If I can't ride my horse, I can at least ride a bicycle, and maybe later, I'll get in a good round of golf."

"What a strange bicycle shop," he thought as he entered. As he looked around, he saw bicycle tires, seats, handlebars, pedals and chains all scattered around the floor. But not a bicycle frame was in sight!

"I wish I could explain it," a young man said, surprising Dr. Smith. "I'm sorry, I didn't mean to startle you. I thought you were the police.

When I got in this morning, the store was just like this. It's as if some practical joker came in and took nothing but the frames. Now what can we do — a bicycle rental shop, with no bicycle frames." (Bicycle Frame - I. R. Johnson)

**Stephen E. Randall**

Thoroughly confused, Dr. Smith pulled back out into traffic, and headed directly for the Lakewood Pines Golf Course. "If I can't do anything else, at least I can get in a few holes before the day is out."

As he headed to the first tee, Dr. Smith reached into his golf bag to get his driver. Setting the bag down, he reached into the pocket to get a golf ball and tee but something was missing. "I know I put some golf tees in this bag," he murmured to himself. But none were to be found. Even more confused, he put the ball on the grass and prepared to tee off without one. (Golf Tee - George F. Grant)

Just then he heard a loud crash. "Somebody's been hit!" he thought to himself. He dropped the golf club and rushed over to see what happened.

**Calvin Didn't Know**

*Calvin's wish was beginning to affect more and more people as the day progressed ...*

Dr. Smith arrived at the emergency room just before the ambulance. He reached the paramedic just as he was getting out of the car.

"I'll go and get him signed in," Dr. Smith said. "You guys meet me at the elevator."

Stephen E. Randall

With that, Dr. Smith rushed into the hospital. What he noticed when he stepped through the door may have been the strangest sight he had ever seen. The entire hospital was lit with candles and gas lamps. It was as if he stepped into the past. (Electric Lamp - Lewis H. Latimer and Joseph V. Nichols)

**Calvin Didn't Know**

He rushed over to the main desk, grabbed his white jacket and reached for the sign-in tablet. Reaching for his fountain pen, he noticed that it was missing from his coat pocket. "No bother," he thought, reaching down to grab a pencil from the desk.

Strangely enough, each pencil he tried had a broken lead; and the pencil sharpener was nowhere to be found. "Oh forget it," he thought. "I'll take care of that later," he told the desk attendant as he rushed towards the elevator.

On his way to the elevator, Dr. Smith noticed something else strange. Evidently someone had spilled some water on the floor. But instead of using mops, people were on their hands and knees, getting up the water with paper towels. What was going on?

Dr. Smith reached the elevator just as the gurney was rolling up. "We have to get him to the operating room on the sixth floor," he told the Paramedics. "He needs help fast."

Calvin, barely conscious, saw all of this but could not move or respond. It was as if a movie were being played out in his mind. And the voice kept ringing in his ears, "The fountain pen ... the pencil sharpener ... the mop," it echoed.

"Make it stop!" Calvin thought to himself ... "Somebody, please make it stop!" (Fountain Pen - William B. Purvis; Pencil Sharpener - John L. Love; Mop - T. W. Stewart)

When the elevator doors opened, everybody stood in disbelief. The elevator was not there, just an empty shaft. "What has happened to my hospital," cried Dr. Smith.

"You happened!" the voice echoed in Calvin's ears. "You made your wish. Now even the elevator is gone." (Elevator - A. Miles)

Thoroughly confused, Dr. Smith and the paramedics carried Calvin's body up five flights of stairs and into the operating room. As they walked in, Dr. Smith sensed trouble. Just as the rest of the hospital, the operating room was lit with candles and gas lamps. Though not very bright, the light would have to do.

"Get me five pints of blood ... Stat!" Dr. Smith ordered the operating room assistant. "Prepare for surgery," he told the Paramedics. "We'll need every set of hands we can get!"

Suddenly, the operating room assistant rushed back into the room. "You won't believe this doctor," the assistant gasped. "There is no stored blood in the hospital!"

**Calvin Didn't Know**

"Calvin," the voice taunted. "You made your wish, now live with it. There is no stored blood now because of you." (Process for Separating Blood from Plasma - Charles Drew)

Just then, Calvin's heart stopped. "We're losing him!" the assistant yelled. "We need to do something now!"

"We'll have to operate!" Dr. Smith announced. "Get me the latest diagrams on open heart surgery. I want to do this by the book."

"What book," the assistant replied. "The diagrams are gone. What do we do now?"

"You really messed up this time," the voice echoed in Calvin's ears. "The diagrams are gone because there is no open heart surgery." (First Successful Open Heart Surgery - Daniel H. Williams)

"What is going on here?" cried Dr. Smith, circling the room. "What has happened to my hospital?"

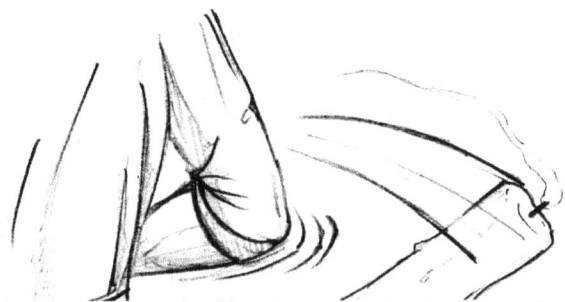

In an attempt to avoid Dr. Smith, the operating room assistant backed up and tripped over a candle, knocking it onto the operating table. Suddenly fire engulfed the table, forcing everyone to take cover.

"The fire extinguisher! Quickly!" screamed Dr. Smith. But it wasn't there. "I give up," an exasperated Dr. Smith finally conceded. "Everybody out. This guy's on his own."

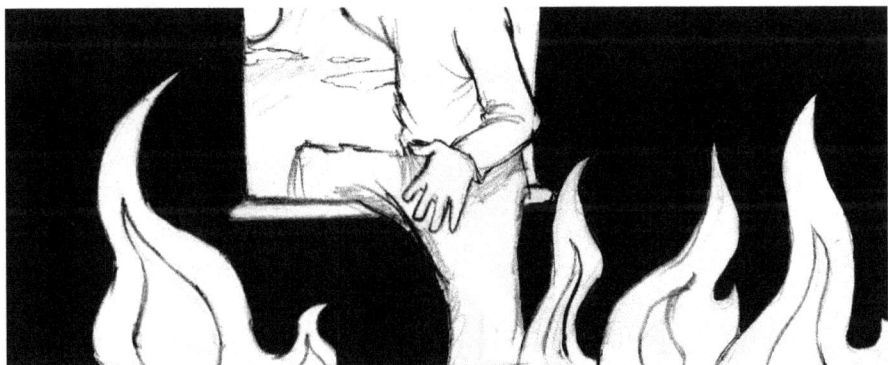

The paramedics, operating room assistant and Dr. Smith all ran from the operating room to the fire escape. They rushed to climb down the ladder, but the ladder was missing. Trapped, they all leaped from the fire escape and fell towards the ground.

**Calvin Didn't Know**

"See what you caused?" the voice told Calvin. "Not only did you hurt yourself, but you've harmed others as well. The fire extinguisher and fire escape ladder are gone now because of you." (Fire Extinguisher - T. J. Marshall; Fire Escape Ladder - R. J. Winters)

So Calvin lay bleeding to death as the fire slowly consumed him. As he began to fade out, scenes from his day played out in his mind. His house in shambles ... no folding bed ... no ironing board ... no clock ... no curtain rod ... no electric lamp ... no thermostat and air conditioner ... no lock ... no lawn sprinkler ... his car changed from an automatic to a stick shift ... the traffic signal gone ... the hospital changed. And each time a voice would tell him that he wouldn't have had these things without African-Americans. "How could I have been so ignorant?" he thought, finally realizing the error of his wish. "I just didn't know, I just didn't know, I just didn't ..."

Stephen E. Randall

# Epilogue

**Calvin Didn't Know**

"I JUST DIDN'T KNOW!!" Calvin screamed as his head hit the floor. He had rolled off the couch bed and landed next to the ironing board.

"Wait, I'm alive!" he yelled as he stood and looked around. Everything was in place, the folding bed ... the ironing board ... the clock ... the curtain rod ... the electric lamp ... the thermostat and air conditioner. He rushed outside to check and sure enough, the lock and the lawn sprinkler were in place. Everything was as it should be.

But everything was not as it should be, he thought. What of this dream? Others must be told of the great things that African Americans have done in this country. "I'll see that they are," Calvin thought seeing African American people in a brand new light, "I'll make certain that they are."

Stephen E. Randall

## GLOSSARY

| | |
|---|---|
| Assemble | to put together |
| Compartment | a separate division |
| Concussion | a severe injury of the head |
| Consume | to do away with |
| Diagram | a scientific drawing |
| Disbelief | a belief that something is untrue |
| Engulf | to flow over |
| Exasperated | extremely bothered |
| Gurney | a wheeled cot or stretcher |
| Incensed | extremely angry |
| Mused | thought |
| Reeling | acting disorderly |
| Refinement | a cleaning process |
| Resolution | the act of solving |
| Stat | immediately |
| Taunt | to mock or challenging |
| Vital | signs medical measurements (pulse temperature, and blood pressure) |
| Warily | cautiously |

**Stephen E. Randall**

# AFRICAN-AMERICAN INVENTIONS AND INVENTORS

Folding Bed                                                Leonard C. Bailey
18 July 1899-Present, Patent # 629,826

Ironing Board                                         Sarah Boone
26 April 1892, Patent # 473,653

Air Conditioner & Thermostat                Frederick M Jones
Air Conditioner, 12 July 1949, Patent #2,475,841
Thermostat, 23 February 1960, Patent #2,926,005

Electric Lamp                                    Lewis H. Latimer &
13 September 1881, Patent #247,097            Joseph V. Nichols

Curtain Rod                                          S. R. Scottron
30 August 1892, Patent # 481,720

First Clock Assembly                           Benjamin Banniker

The Lock                                              W. A. Martin
23 July 1889, Patent # 407,738

Lawn Sprinkler                                    Joseph H. Smith
4 May 1897, Patent # 581,785

Automatic Gear Shift                          Richard B. Spikes
6 December 1932, Patent # 1,889,814

Traffic Signal                                        Garret Morgan
20 November 1923, Patent #1,475,024

Sugar Refinement Process                   Nobert Rillieux
10 December 1846, Patent # 4,879

Horseshoe                                           O. E. Brown
23 August 1892, Patent #481,271

**Calvin Didn't Know**

Saddle  William D. Davis
6 October 1896, Patent # 568,939

Bicycle Frame  Isaac R. Johnson
10 October 1899, Patent #634,823

Golf Tee  George F. Grant
12 December 1899, Patent # 638,920

Mop  T. W. Stewart
13 June 1893, Patent # 499,402

Pencil Sharpener  John L. Love
23 November 1897, Patent #419,065

Elevator  A. Miles
11 October 1887, Patent #371,207

Process for Separating Plasma from Blood  Charles Drew

First Successful Open Heart Surgery  Daniel H. Williams
10 July 1893

Fire Extinguisher  T. J. Marshall
26 May 1872, Patent #125,063

Fire Escape Ladder  R. J. Winters
7 May 1878, Patent #203,517

Stephen E. Randall

# Biographies of Selected Inventors
## Benjamin Banneker

Inventor, Mathematician, Almanac Maker

Benjamin Banneker was a self-educated scientist, astronomer, inventor, writer, and antislavery publicist. He built a striking clock entirely from wood, published a Farmers' Almanac, and actively campaigned against slavery. He was one of the first African Americans to gain distinction in science.

On November 9 1731, Benjamin Banneker was born in Ellicott's Mills, Maryland. He was the descendent of slaves, however, Banneker was born a freeman. At that time the law dictated that if your mother was a slave then you were a slave, and if she was a freewomen then you were a free person. Banneker's grandmother, Molly Walsh was a bi-racial English immigrant and indentured servant who married an African slave named Banna Ka, who had been brought to the Colonies by a slave trader. Molly had served seven years as an indentured servant before she acquired and worked on her own small farm. Molly Walsh purchased her future husband Banna Ka and another African to work on her farm. The name Banna Ka was later changed to Bannaky and then changed to Banneker. Benjamin's mother Mary Banneker was born free. Benjamin's father Rodger was a former slave who had bought his own freedom before marrying Mary.

Benjamin Banneker was educated by Quakers, however, most of his education was self-taught. He quickly revealed to the world his inventive nature and first achieved national acclaim for his scientific work in the 1791 survey of the Federal Territory (now Washington, D.C.). In 1753, he built the first watch made in America, a wooden pocket watch. Twenty years later, Banneker began making astronomical calculations that enabled him to successfully forecast a 1789 solar eclipse. His estimate made well in advance of the celestial event, contradicted predictions of better-known mathematicians and astronomers.

Banneker's mechanical and mathematical abilities impressed many, including Thomas Jefferson who encountered Banneker after George

### Calvin Didn't Know

Elliot had recommended him for the surveying committee that laid out Washington D.C. When the chairman of the committee, Major L'Enfant, abruptly resigned and returned to France with his plans, Banneker's precise memory enabled him to reproduce the plans in their entirety.

Banneker is best known for his six annual Farmer's Almanacs published between 1792 and 1797. In his free time, Banneker began compiling the Pennsylvania, Delaware, Maryland, and Virginia Almanac and Ephemeris. The almanacs included information on medicines and medical treatment, and listed tides, astronomical information, and eclipses, all calculated by Banneker himself.

On August 19 1791, Banneker sent a copy of his first almanac to secretary of state Thomas Jefferson. In an enclosed letter, he questioned the slaveholder's sincerity as a "friend to liberty." He urged Jefferson to help get rid of "absurd and false ideas" that one race is superior to another. He wished Jefferson's sentiments to be the same as his, that "one Universal Father ... afforded us all the same sensations and endowed us all with the same faculties." Jefferson responded with praise for Banneker's accomplishments.

Benjamin Banneker died on October 25, 1806.

Stephen E. Randall

# Charles Drew

Physician; Blood Plasma Researcher

Charles Drew was born June 3, 1904, to Richard and Nora Drew, the oldest of five children. He attended Dunbar High School in Washington, D.C. becoming best known as an athlete. He received the James E. Walker Memorial Medal for all-around athletic performance. At Amherst College, he was a star quarterback, the most valuable baseball player, captain of the track team, and national high hurdles champion. He received the Howard Hill Mossman Trophy as the man who had contributed the most to athletics during his four years at Amherst.

For two years after college, Charles took a job as athletic director, football coach, and science instructor at Morgan State College in Baltimore. In 1928, he entered medical school at McGill University in Montreal, Canada.

Charles Drew continued to excell in sports at McGill, just as he had at Amherst. Drew joined Dr. John Beattie, a British professor, in doing blood research. He found it fascinating and decided to give further attention to it. During his two years at Montreal General Hospital, as an intern and resident doctor, he continued his research on blood.

Drew received a fellowship for specialized advanced training from Howard University's Medical School, making it possible for him to study at Columbia University Medical School. Drew's assignment was to learn all he could about collecting and storing blood until it was needed for transfusions. He experimented with blood plasma and discovered that it could be used instead of whole blood. It lasted longer and was less likely to become contaminated. Dr. Drew published his findings in an article called "Banked Blood," since the process of collecting and storing blood was called "banking" it.

Dr. Drew earned his Doctor of Medical Science degree from Columbia University in 1940. This was also the start of World War II. Drew and other American blood specialists were exploring ways to get life-saving blood plasma to the war front when Charles received an urgent request from his former teacher, Dr. John Beattie, who had returned to England. A cablegram asked for 5,000 ampules of dried plasma for transfusions, plus the same amount three weeks later. Dr. Drew was chosen medical supervisor of the "Blood for Britain" project, which helped save the lives of many wounded soldiers.

Following this success, Charles Drew was named director of the Red Cross Blood Bank and assistant director of the National Research Council, in charge of blood collection for the U.S. Army and Navy. As Drew set up the blood bank and trained staff, he also spoke out against the armed forces' directive that blood was to be separated according to the race of the donor. Dr. Drew knew this was wrong, that there was no racial difference in blood. Soldiers and sailors would die needlessly if they had to wait for "same race" blood.

Then on April 1, 1950 while driving to the Andrew Memorial Clinic in Tuskegee, Alabama to deliver the annual lecture, Dr. Drew dozed off as he drove. The car ran off the road and turned over. Drew was badly injured.

Newspaper accounts said that the hospital nearest the accident refused to admit Dr. Drew because of his race, and that precious time was lost in taking him farther down the road to a black hospital. By the time he arrived there, he had lost so much blood that no one could have saved his life. It seemed a cruel hoax that the man who had done more than anyone else in the world to make blood transfusions available to people in emergency situations did not have access to a blood transfusion when he needed it.

According to Dr. Ford (another black physician who was with Dr. Drew in the accident), "Doctor Drew's cause of death was that of a broken neck and complete blockage of the blood flow back to the heart. In the accident, he was half thrown out of the car and actually crushed to death by the car as it rolled over."

Stephen E. Randall

## George F. Grant

Golf Tee, 12 Dec 1899, #638,920

George Franklin Grant was born in Oswego, New York in 1847 and was the son of former slaves. He graduated from Harvard Dental School in 1870. He was one of two African Americans to first graduate from Harvard Dental school, where he later taught.

An avid golfer, Gorge was also interested in the physics of golfing. He set about to improve the game of golf and as a result he received U.S. patent No. 638,920 on December 12, 1899 for an improved golf tee. It was the world's first patent for a golf tee.

The golf tee was a small wooden peg with a concave top which held the ball in place while the golfer drove the ball for long distances. Prior to Grant's invention, the player would place the ball on the ground and hope that it would not roll away. This, as you might imagine, did not work too well. Most of the time the players would find themselves digging up the turf while trying to hit the ball. Today, many people around the world enjoy playing golf, thanks to George F. Grant's golf tee concept and invention.

George Grant was also recognized internationally for his invention of the oblate palate, a prosthetic device he designed for treatment of the cleft palate.

**Calvin Didn't Know**

## Frederick McKinley Jones

Technician
Air Conditioning Unit, 12 Jul 1949, #2,475,841;
Thermostat and Temperature Control System, 23 Feb 1960, #2,926,005

Frederick M. Jones was born in Covington, Kentucky on May 17, 1892 or 1893, to an Irish father, John Jones and an African American mother who abandoned the family soon after her son was born.

The Jones family struggled in poverty, as permanent work was hard to find and John Jones was challenged with the responsibility of caring for a small child and holding a job. He was constantly exasperated by Jones' method of learning how mechanical machinery worked—he always took things apart.

When Jones was seven years old, his father sent him to live and be educated at the local Catholic church. Father Ryan, a Catholic priest, cared for Jones and encouraged his interest in mechanics. Jones helped around the church and rectory with cleaning, cooking, maintenance, and grounds work, but he never found a home there. Jones's father died when he was nine.

Jones eventually rebelled against the structure and rules of Catholic school and never settled happily there, finding it repetitious and boring. He was 11 years old when he dropped out of school and ran away. Jones crossed the river and went back to Cincinnati, immediately picking up employment at an auto garage. The young Jones had a love of the mechanics of cars, and strove to spend as much time learning about autos as possible. He was hired to keep the garage clean but soon demonstrated his natural capability as a mechanic. Jones worked full-time as a mechanic in the garage upon turning 14. By the time he was 15, Jones supervised the garage as mechanic foreman. He also became passionately interested in racecar driving, and assisted the owner of the garage with building racing cars. After a dispute which involved Jones going to the racetrack during work hours, Jones was fired at the age of 19.

In 1913, Jones was working as a janitor and repair person for a Minneapolis hotel. A visiting guest, Oscar Younggren, took notice of Jones' ability in repairing a boiler and asked if he would like to serve as a mechanic on

Younggren's 50,000-acre family farm. Jones relocated to Hallock and worked on the farm, in charge of maintaining and repairing all machinery and cars. When the farm was sold two years later, Jones remained in the area, finding work repairing cars. He remained in Hallock for the next 18 years, leaving only for World War I.

Returning from France after serving in World War I, Jones moved back to Hallock and continued to work on mechanical projects. He was the town's movie projectionist and in the late 1920's, designed a series of devices for the developing movie industry, which adapted silent movie projectors to use talking movie stock.. As film technology continued to change, Jones developed movie sound technology that cost less and performed better than comparable products on the market. With his experience as a mechanic he also developed a self-starting gasoline motor and an apparatus for the movie box-office that delivers tickets and returns change to customers.

Jones' inventions to develop quality movie soundtrack mechanics caused entrepreneur Joseph A. Numero of Minneapolis, to notice the young mechanic's skills. Numero's Minneapolis based company was experiencing difficulty keeping up with the rapid changes in motion picture equipment. So he employed Jones to improve the quality of the sound equipment that the company manufactured. Jones's sound track inventions propelled Numero's company to the forefront of the industry. On June 17, 1939, Jones was granted his first patent for a movie theater ticket machine.

On a hot summer night in 1937 in Minneapolis, Minnesota, Frederick Jones was driving around a lake wondering why no one invented air conditioning for cars and trucks. The next morning Frederick Jones went to the library to look up information on refrigeration and air conditioning. After finding some information, Jones then went to work on a sketch for a car air conditioner. Jones decided to show his plans to his boss Joseph A. Numero, who decided that he was not interested. Numero thought it was too heavy and expensive to make. So Jones left his idea alone for a while, but not for long. Some time later, Numero's business peer, Harry Werner, complained during a game of golf, that he was unable to ship food without it perishing. Numero jokingly remarked that Werner needed a refrigerator for his truck, never expecting to be taken seriously. However, Werner purchased an aluminum truck and brought it to Numero and Jones for consideration. Numero thought that the project was impossible, but Jones got into the truck, took some measurements, and quickly concluded that a refrigeration unit could be developed. After some experimentation, Jones developed a refrigeration unit that could withstand shock and could mount to the forehead of a truck. He patented this invention on July 12, 1940. The system was, in turn, adapted to a variety of other common carriers, including ships and railway cars.

Numero eventually sold Cinema Supplies, Inc. to RCA in order to form a partnership with Jones. Jones and Numero called their new company the U.S. Thermo Control Company. It was later known as the Thermo King Corporation. The partnership went on to earn $3 million by 1949 and in the late 1990s, was still a familiar name and a major contributor to the refrigeration industry.

Jones' productive career yielded 61 patents. Forty of these involved refrigeration systems, but Jones also invented portable X-ray equipment, audio equipment, and engines. But not all his inventions were patented by him, the condenser microphone and portable X-ray machine were eventually patented and manufactured by other persons.

Jones was married twice. His first marriage, to a Swedish woman from Hallock, lasted just a few years until he moved to Minneapolis. His 1946 marriage to his second wife, Lucille, lasted until his death.

Jones died of lung cancer on February 21, 1961 in Minneapolis and was buried at Fort Snelling National Cemetery. He was inducted into the Minnesota Inventors Hall of Fame in 1977.

Stephen E. Randall

## Lewis Howard Latimer

Electric Lamp (w/ Joseph Nichols), 13 Sep 1881, #247, 097

Lewis Latimer was born in Chelsea, Massachusetts in 1848. He was the son of George and Rebecca Latimer, escaped slaves from Virginia. When Lewis Latimer was a boy his father George was arrested and tried as a slave fugitive. The judge ordered his return to Virginia and slavery, but money was raised by the local community to pay for George Latimer's freedom. George Latimer later went underground fearing his re-enslavement, a great hardship for Lewis' family.

Lewis Latimer enlisted in the Union Navy at the age of 15 by forging the age on his birth certificate. Upon the completion of his military service, Lewis Latimer returned to Boston, Massachusetts where he was employed by the patent solicitors Crosby & Gould. While working in the office Lewis began the study of drafting and eventually became their head draftsmen. During his employment with Crosby & Gould, Latimer drafted the patent drawings for Alexander Graham Bell's patent application for the telephone, spending long nights with the inventor. Bell rushed his patent application to the patent office mere hours ahead of the competition and won the patent rights to the telephone with the help of Latimer.

Hiram S. Maxim, founder of the U.S. Electric Light Co., at Bridgeport, CN, and the inventor of the Maxim machine gun, hired Lewis Latimer as an assistant manager and draftsman. Latimer's talent for drafting and his creative genius led him to invent a method of making carbon filaments for the Maxim electric incandescent lamp. In 1881, he supervised the installation of the electric lights in New York, Philadelphia, Montreal, and London.

Lewis Latimer was the original draftsman for Thomas Edison (who he started working for in 1884) and as such was the star witness in Edison's infringement suits. Lewis Latimer was the only African American member of the twenty-four "Edison Pioneers", Thomas Edison's engineering division of the Edison Company. Latimer also co-authored a book on electricity published in 1890 called, "Incandescent Electric Lighting: A Practical Description of the Edison System."

**Calvin Didn't Know**

Lewis Latimer had many interests. He was an inventor, draftsman, engineer, author, poet, musician, and, at the same time, a devoted family man and philanthropist. He married Mary Wilson on December 10, 1873. Lewis wrote a poem for his wedding entitled Ebon Venus that was published in his book of poetry, Poems of Love and Life. The Latimers had two daughters, Jeanette and Louise.

# John L. Love

Pencil Sharpener, 23 Nov 1897, #594,114

The "Love Sharpener", was designed by John Lee Love of Fall River, MA. Love's invention was the very simple, portable pencil sharpener that many artists use, the pencil is put into the opening of the sharpener and rotated by hand, and the shavings stay inside the sharpener. Love's sharpener was patented on November 23, 1897 (U.S. Patent # 594,114). Four years earlier, Love created and patented his first invention the "Plasterer's Hawk." This device which is still used today, is a flat square piece of board made of wood or metal, upon which plaster or mortar was placed and then spread by plasterers or masons. This was patented on July 9, 1895.

Calvin Didn't Know

## A. Miles

Elevator, 11 Oct 1887, #371,207

Alexander Miles of Duluth, Minnesota patented an electric elevator (U.S. pat#371,207) on October 11, 1887. Alexander Miles did not invent the first elevator, however, his design was very important. His design improved the method of the opening and closing of elevator doors; and he improved the closing of the opening to the elevator shaft when an elevator was not on that floor. Alexander Miles created an automatic mechanism that closed access to the shaft. At that time elevator patrons or operators were often required to manually shut a door to cutoff access to the elevator shaft. People would forget to close the shaft door and as a result there were accidents with people falling down the elevator shafts.

Stephen E. Randall

## Garrett A. Morgan

Traffic Signal, 20 Nov 1923, #1,475,024

Garrett Morgan was an inventor and businessman from Cleveland who invented a device called the Morgan safety hood and smoke protector in 1914. On July 25, 1916, Garrett Morgan made national news for using his gas mask to rescue 32 men trapped during an explosion in an underground tunnel 250 feet beneath Lake Erie. Morgan and a team of volunteers donned the new "gas masks" and went to the rescue. After the rescue, Morgan's company received requests from fire departments around the country who wished to purchase the new masks. The Morgan gas mask was later refined for use by U.S. Army during World War I. In 1914, Garrett Morgan was awarded a patent for a Safety Hood and Smoke Protector. Two years later, a refined model of his early gas mask won a gold medal at the International Exposition of Sanitation and Safety, and another gold medal from the International Association of Fire Chiefs.

The son of former slaves, Garrett Morgan was born in Paris, Kentucky on March 4, 1877. His early childhood was spent attending school and working on the family farm with his brothers and sisters. While still a teenager, he left Kentucky and moved north to Cincinnati, Ohio in search of opportunity.

Although Garrett Morgan's formal education never took him beyond elementary school, he hired a tutor while living in Cincinnati and continued his studies in English grammar. In 1895, Morgan moved to Cleveland, Ohio, where he went to work as a sewing machine repair man for a clothing manufacturer. News of his proficiency for fixing things and experimenting traveled fast and led to numerous job offers from various manufacturing firms in the Cleveland area.

In 1907, the inventor opened his own sewing equipment and repair shop. It was the first of several businesses he would establish. In 1909, he expanded the enterprise to include a tailoring shop that employed 32 employees. The new company turned out coats, suits and dresses, all sewn with equipment that Garrett Morgan himself had made.

**Calvin Didn't Know**

In 1920, Garrett Morgan moved into the newspaper business when he established the Cleveland Call. As the years went on, he became a prosperous and widely respected business man, and he was able to purchase a home and an automobile. Indeed it was Morgan's experience while driving along the streets of Cleveland that inspired him to invent an improvement to traffic signals.

The first American-made automobiles were introduced to U.S. consumers shortly before the turn of the century. The Ford Motor Company was founded in 1903 and with it American consumers began to discover the adventures of the open road. In the early years of the 20th century it was not uncommon for bicycles, animal-powered wagons, and new gasoline-powered motor vehicles to share the same streets and roadways with pedestrians. Accidents were frequent. After witnessing a collision between an automobile and a horse-drawn carriage, Garrett Morgan took his turn at inventing a traffic signal. Other inventors had experimented with, marketed, and even patented traffic signals, however, Garrett Morgan was one of the first to apply for and acquire a U.S. patent for an inexpensive to produce traffic signal. The patent was granted on November 20, 1923. Garrett Morgan also had his invention patented in Great Britain and Canada.

Garrett Morgan stated in his patent for the traffic signal, "This invention relates to traffic signals, and particularly to those which are adapted to be positioned adjacent the intersection of two or more streets and are manually operable for directing the flow of traffic... In addition, my invention contemplates the provision of a signal which may be readily and cheaply manufactured."

The Morgan traffic signal was a T-shaped pole unit that featured three positions: Stop, Go and an all-directional stop position. This "third position" halted traffic in all directions to allow pedestrians to cross streets more safely.

Garrett Morgan's hand-cranked semaphore traffic management device was in use throughout North America until all manual traffic signals were replaced by the automatic red, yellow, and green-light traffic signals currently used around the world. The inventor sold the rights to his traffic signal to the General Electric Corporation for $40,000. Shortly before his death in 1963, Garrett Morgan was awarded a citation for his traffic signal by the United States Government.

Garrett Morgan was constantly experimenting to develop new concepts. Though the traffic signal came at the height of his career and became one of his most renowned inventions, it was just one of several innovations he developed, manufactured, and sold over the years.

Morgan invented a zig-zag stitching attachment for manually operated sewing machine. He also founded a company that made personal grooming products, such as hair dying ointments and the curved-tooth pressing comb.

As word of Garrett Morgan's life-saving inventions spread across North America and England, demand for these products grew. He was frequently invited to conventions and public exhibitions to demonstrate how his inventions worked.

Garrett Morgan died on August 27, 1963, at the age of 86. His life was long and full, and his creative energies have given us a marvelous and lasting legacy.

**Calvin Didn't Know**

## William B. Purvis

Fountain Pen, 07 Jan 1890, #419,065

William Purvis of Philadelphia invented and patented improvements to the fountain pen in 1890. William Purvis made several improvements to the fountain pen in order to make a "more durable, inexpensive, and better pen to carry in the pocket." Purvis used an elastic tube between the pen nib and the ink reservoir that used a suction action to return any excess ink to the ink reservoir, reducing ink spills and increasing the longevity of the ink. Fountain pens were first patented as early as 1809.

William Purvis also invented several other inventions including two machines for making paper bags (which Purvis sold to the Union Paper Bag Company of New York), a bag fastener, a self-inking hand stamp, and several devices for electric railroads. His first paper bag machine (patent #293,353) created satchel bottom type bags in an improved volume and greater automation than previous machines.

Stephen E. Randall

## Norbert Rilleux

Sugar Refiner (evaporating pan), 10 Dec 1846, #4879

Norbert Rillieux was born the son of a wealthy, white New Orleans plantation owner and his black slave mistress. At Norbert's birth, his father had the choice of declaring him free or, as was the custom in such instances, a slave.

Thankfully for Norbert, his father broke tradition and made him free, entitling him to education and privileges usually reserved for entirely white people. Growing up, he took great interest in the workings of the plantation and witnessed the inefficiency of the sugar-making process and the brutal labor that slaves endured in it.

Sugar cane juice was heated in a series of open kettles and pans called the "Jamaica Train," where slaves poured juice from container to container with long-handled ladles. The work was hard, hot and dangerous.

Studying engineering in Paris, Rillieux learned that the boiling point of liquids is reduced as atmospheric pressure is reduced. This made Rillieux think that the evaporation of sugar on his father's plantation could be done more efficiently if the cane juice was heated in a vacuum. He also thought that the steam from one vessel could be used to heat the juice in the next vessel.

The invention he came up with and patented — the multiple effect pan evaporator — was a great success. Not only did it make better sugar, but it saved countless workers around the world from working in highly dangerous conditions.

When his evaporator process was finally adopted in Europe, he returned to inventing with renewed interest—applying his process to the sugar beet. In so doing, he cut production and refining costs in half.

Rillieux died in Paris on October 8, 1894, leaving behind a system which is in universal use throughout the sugar industry, as well as in the manufacture of soap, geletin, glue, and many other products.

**Calvin Didn't Know**

# Joseph H. Smith

Lawn Sprinkler, 04 May 1897, #581,785

Joseph Smith received a patent for his lawn sprinkler invention on May 4, 1897. Smith's lawn sprinkler was a swivel-shaped device containing a core which distributed water over a wide area. Previously, most lawns were watered with hand-held hoses. Because of their labor-saving advantages, today lawn sprinklers are used by homeowners and others the world over.

Stephen E. Randall

## Richard B. Spikes

Automatic Gear Shift, 06 Dec 1932, #1,889,814;
Transmission and Shifting Thereof, 28 Nov 1933, #1,936,996

Richard Spikes of San Francisco, California patented an improved automatic gear shift in 1932. His object was to develop a gear shift where the gears for the various speeds were in constant mesh. Richard Spikes invented a novel clutch mechanism for his gear shift, he used levers to shift gears.

Richard Spikes also patented or developed the following inventions:

Railroad semaphore (1906)
Automatic car washer (1913)
Automobile directional signals (1913) - manufactured by Pierce Arrow
Beer keg tap (1910) - purchased by Milwaukee Brewing Company.
Self-locking rack for billiard cues (1910)
Continuous contact trolley pole (1919) - used on on the famous San Francisco Key Line.
Combination milk bottle opener and cover (1926)
Method and apparatus for obtaining average samples and temperature of tank liquids (1931)
Improved automatic gear shift (1932) - licensed the patent for $100,000
Transmission and shifting thereof (1933)
Automatic shoe shine chair (1939)
Multiple barrel machine gun (1940)
Horizontally swinging barber chair (1950)
Automatic safety brake (1962) - year Richard Spikes died.

While Richard Spikes was working on his automatic safety brake in 1962, he lost his vision. As a result, Richard Spikes designed a drafting machine for blind people, in order to assist him in his inventing.

Calvin Didn't Know

## Daniel Hale Williams

First Successful Open Heart Surgery
July 10, 1893

At Provident Hospital in 1893, Dr. Williams performed the operation upon which his later fame rests. On July 10 of that year, a patient was admitted to the emergency ward with a knife wound in an artery lying a fraction of an inch from the heart. With the aid of six staff surgeons, Williams made an incision in the patient's chest and operated successfully on the artery.

For the next four days, the patient, James Cornish, lay near death, his temperature far above normal and his pulse dangerously uneven. An encouraging rally then brought him out of immediate danger, terminating the crisis period. Three weeks later, minor surgery was performed by Dr. Williams to remove fluid from Cornish's pleural cavity. After recuperating for still another month, Cornish fully recovered and was able to leave the hospital, scarred but cured.

An uproar of publicity greeted Dr. Williams's later announcement that his heart surgery had been successful. Much of it was negative, in the sense that skeptics doubted that a black doctor could engineer such a significant breakthrough. Unaffected by the notoriety, Williams continued a full-time association with Freedman's Hospital, which he headed, prior to the founding of Provident Hospital.

Dr. Williams died in 1931 after a lifetime devoted to his two main interests— the NAACP and the construction of hospitals and training schools for black doctors and nurses.

**Stephen E. Randall**

**Calvin Didn't Know**

# ORDER MORE BETTER DAY TITLES

**Titles:**

| | | |
|---|---|---|
| Zora's Valentine | (978-0-9767189-0-1) | $13.00 |
| Calvin Didn't Know | (978-9767189-3-2) | $13.00 |
| Ralph's Bugle | (978-9767189-2-5) | $13.00 |
| The Chocolate Moose | (978-9767189-5-6) | $13.00 |
| Where the Heart Is | (978-9767189-4-9) | $13.00 |

*Shipping Address* _____

*City* _____ *State* _____ *Zip Code* _____

*Contact Person* _____ *Phone* _____

*Payment Method:*   ☐ Visa   ☐ Master Card   ☐ Money Order

▢▢▢▢▢▢▢▢▢▢▢▢▢▢▢▢   ▢▢▢▢
*Credit Card Number*   *Exp. Date*

_____
*Card Holders Signature*

| ISBN # | Book Title | Quantity | Price | Shipping $6.95 |
|---|---|---|---|---|
| | | | | |
| | | | | |
| | | | | |
| | | | | |
| | | | | |
| | | | | |
| | | | | |

*Mail to:*
*Better Day Publishing, LLC*
*11152 Westheimer #341*
*Houston, Texas 77042*

*"Bridging Minds to Better Days!"*

**Calvin Didn't Know**

**Stephen E. Randall**

**Calvin Didn't Know**

www.ingramcontent.com/pod-product-compliance
Lightning Source LLC
Chambersburg PA
CBHW051708090426
42736CB00013B/2603